LEARN TO DRAW
BASIC DRAWING COURSE: from A to Z
Copyright © Giuseppe Lombardi
www.fattidisegnare.com

Tutti i diritti riservati.
La violazione dei diritti riservati può comportare sanzioni legali e quindi se si vuole utilizzare il contenuto del libro protetto da diritti d'autore è necessario ottenere il permesso dall'autore o dal proprietario del copyright."

All rights reserved. Violation of reserved rights may result in legal sanctions, and therefore, if you wish to use the content of the book protected by copyright, it is necessary to obtain permission from the author or the copyright owner.

Todos los derechos reservados. La violación de los derechos reservados puede conllevar sanciones legales y, por lo tanto, si se desea utilizar el contenido del libro protegido por derechos de autor, es necesario obtener permiso del autor o del propietario del copyright.

Tous droits réservés. La violation des droits réservés peut entraîner des sanctions légales et donc, si vous souhaitez utiliser le contenu du livre protégé par le droit d'auteur, il est nécessaire d'obtenir la permission de l'auteur ou du propriétaire du copyright.

Все права защищены. Нарушение защищенных прав может повлечь за собой юридические санкции, и поэтому, если вы хотите использовать содержание книги, защищенной авторским правом, необходимо получить разрешение от автора или владельца авторских прав.

LEARN TO DRAW
BASIC DRAWING COURSE: From A to Z

INDEX

Intro _____ 5

Chapter 1: Introduction to Design _____ 6
1.1 Basic materials
 - Introduction to drawing tools: pencils, erasers, pencil sharpeners, paper.
 - Importance of posture and lighting.

1.2 Basic lines and shapes _____ 8
 - Straight and curved line drawing exercises.
 - Drawing simple geometric shapes (circles, squares, triangles).

1.3 Hand control _____ 11
 - Precision exercises: hatching and shading.
 - Design of repetitive shapes to improve control.

Chapter 2: Observation and Proportions _____ 14
2.1 Active observation
 - Learning to observe details.
 - Life drawing exercises: simple objects.

2.2 Proportions _____ 16
 - Study of proportions in basic forms.
 - Exercises on how to measure and transpose proportions on the sheet.

2.3 The grid and the squares method _____20
  - Use of the grid to maintain proportions.
  - Exercises in transposing an image using a grid.

Chapter 3: Light and Shadows _____23
3.1 Theory of light and shadow
  - How light interacts with objects.
  - Types of shadows: own shadows and brought shadows.

3.2 Shading of simple shapes _____25
  - Shading and hatching techniques.
  - Practical exercises on geometric shapes.

3.3 Volume and depth _____28
  - Creating the illusion of three-dimensionality.
  - Drawing of complex objects with light and shadow.

Chapter 4: Perspective _____32
4.1 Linear perspective
  - Basic concepts of perspective (vanishing point, horizon line).
  - Drawing of shapes in one-point perspective.

4.2 Two-point perspective _____34
  - Application of two-point perspective.
  - Drawing of more complex objects and environments.

4.3 Atmospheric perspective _____39
  - Use of tonal values to create depth.
  - Practical exercises with landscapes.

Chapter 5: Drawing Objects and Still Life _____43

5.1 Drawing everyday objects
- Study of textures and details.
- Exercises on everyday objects.

5.2 Composition of a still life _____45
- Composition and balancing of elements.
- Drawing of a still life with various objects.

5.3 Colour in still life _____48
- Introduction to colours and colouring techniques.
- Use of colour to enhance drawing.

Chapter 6: Human Body Design _____49

6.1 Basic anatomy
- Proportions of the human body.
- Drawing of stylised figures.

6.2 Study of body parts _____57
- Drawing of hands, feet, face.
- Practical exercises for each part of the body.

6.3 Moving figures _____68
- Drawing dynamic poses.
- Study of movement and balance.

Intro

Drawing is an art form that has the power to transform the way we see the world. Through the study of lines, shapes, shadows and proportions, we learn to carefully observe our surroundings and translate our perceptions into visual images. Each chapter of this book has been carefully structured to address a specific aspect of drawing, starting with the essential tools and continuing with more sophisticated techniques, such as perspective and drawing the human body.

In the first chapter, you will dive into the exploration of basic materials and techniques. Next, you will go through exercises that will help you improve your hand control and develop a keen eye for proportion and detail. As the book progresses, you will discover how to create volume and depth in your drawings, using light and shadow to make your works realistic.

Immerse yourself in this creative journey with curiosity and passion, knowing that each stroke, each line and each shadow represents a step forward in your artistic journey.

Enjoy reading and drawing!

Chapter 1: Introduction to design

1.1 Materials from base

Introduction to drawing tools

Pencils

Pencils are the main tool for drawing.

There are different gradations indicating the hardness or softness of the lead:

- H (Hard) are the hard pencils (H, 2H, 3H, etc.), they produce lighter, thinner lines and are ideal for detailed drawings and light guidelines;
- B (Black) are the soft pencils (B, 2B, 3B, etc.), produce dark, intentional lines and are perfect for shading and more expressive drawings;
- HB are somewhere between H and B, good for general design.

H (Hard)	B (Black)	HB
H	B	HB
2H	2B	
3H	3B	

Tyres

Erasers are essential for correcting errors and creating lighting effects:

- the normal eraser is ideal for erasing large areas;
- the bread rubber is very flexible and perfect for gently removing graphite without damaging the paper.

Gomma normale — Area cancellata   Gomma pane — Sfumatura schiarita

Pencil Sharpener

A good pencil sharpener keeps pencils sharp, allowing precise and detailed lines. There are manual and electric pencil sharpeners.

Paper

The choice of paper can greatly influence the final result:
- sketch paper is generally lighter, ideal for preliminary drawings;
- drawing paper is heavier and with a texture that holds graphite better, perfect for finished works.

Importance of posture and lighting

Posture

Good posture prevents pain and fatigue when drawing. Here are some tips:
- correct sitting with a straight back and feet resting on the ground.
- arms should be relaxed and elbows level with the table.

Lighting

Good lighting reduces eye fatigue and improves visibility at work:
- natural light from a window is ideal, preferably from the side of the dominant hand to avoid shadows on the sheet;
- Artificial light from a white table lamp and positioned so that it does not create disturbing reflections or shadows.

1.2 Lines and shapes of base

This section is essential for developing mastery of basic lines and shapes. Constant practice of these exercises will help you improve your hand control and precision, which are essential for the next sections.

Drawing exercises for straight lines and curves

Straight lines

Drawing straight lines may seem simple, but it requires hand control and precision.

Here are some exercises to practise.

- Parallel lines

Draw several parallel lines maintaining the same distance between them.
Start with short lines and increas gradually increase the length.

- Line grid

Create a grid by drawing horizontal and vertical lines.
This exercise helps you improve precision and control.

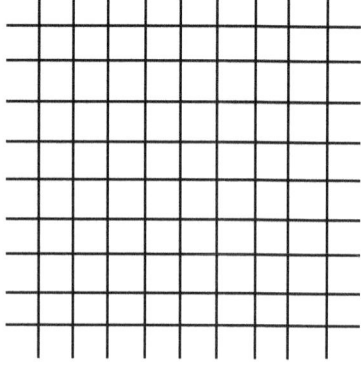

Curved lines

Curved lines require flexibility and fluidity of movement.
Here are some exercises.

- Wavy lines

He draws wavy lines, looking
to maintain a constant rhythm and fluidity.

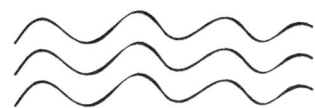

- Concentric circles

Draw concentric circles, starting with a
small circle in the centre and increasing
gradually the size of the outer circles, always try
to keep the same distance.

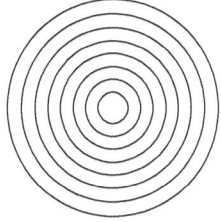

Drawing simple geometric shapes

Circles

Drawing perfect circles freehand can be difficult, but with practice it becomes easier.
Here are some suggestions.

- Points of reference

Draw light cross-shaped reference
points to help you maintain the
symmetry of the circle.

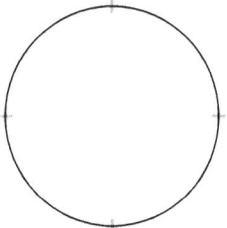

- Smooth movement

Use a fluid wrist movement to trace the circle, keeping your hand relaxed.

Squares

Squares require precision and control of straight lines. Here is how to draw them.

- Tracing the sides
Draw four sides of equal length while maintaining 90 degree angles.

- Symmetry verification
Check that all sides are equal and that the angles are right angles, using a ruler if necessary.

Triangles

Triangles are useful for practising drawing straight lines and angles. Here is how to draw them.

- Equilateral triangle
Draw an equilateral triangle with three sides of equal length. Start with the base and then trace the two remaining sides.

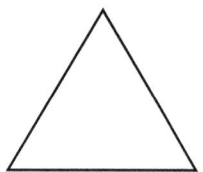

- Isosceles triangle
Draw an isosceles triangle with two sides of equal length. The base will be different.

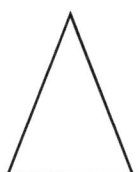

1.3 Control of hand

These exercises are crucial for developing hand control, precision and fluidity in drawing. By practising them regularly, you will improve your ability to create precise lines and shadows, which are essential for progressing to more advanced drawing techniques.

Precision exercises: hatching and shading Hatching
Hatching is a fundamental technique in drawing to create texture and shadows. Here are some exercises to practise it.

- Linear hatching
Draw a series of parallel lines
to create a homogeneous area.
The lines should be close and uniform.

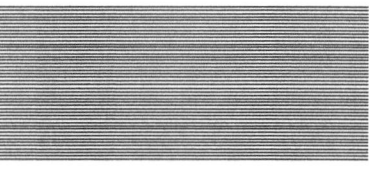

- Cross-hatching Overlap series of
parallel lines
crossing each other to create a darker
shadow. You can use different angles to
intensify the effect.

- Wave hatching
Draw parallel wavy lines for
a softer shading effect.
This technique is useful for creating
organic textures.

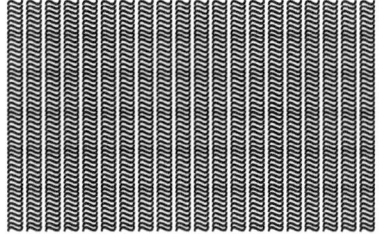

Shading

Shading helps give depth and volume to drawings. Here are some exercises.

- Shadow gradient

Draw a rectangle and create an even gradient from black to white using a hatching or shading technique.

- Shading a sphere Draw a sphere and practice shading to create the illusion of three-dimensionality. It identifies the light source and draws its own shadows and shadows cast.

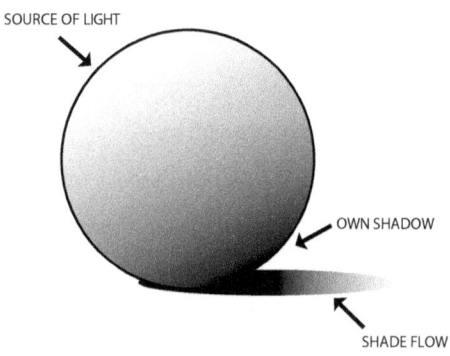

Designing repetitive shapes to improve control

Drawing repetitive shapes is an excellent exercise to improve hand control and accuracy.

- Spirals

It draws concentric spirals, maintaining an even distance between the lines.
This exercise helps develop fluidity of movement.

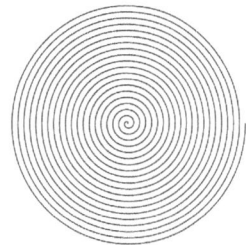

- Geometric motifs
Draw a grid and fill each square with a repetitive geometric pattern, such as circles, triangles or squares.

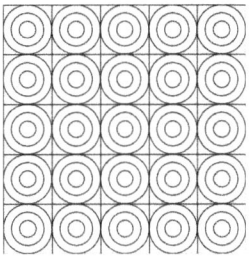

- Drawing ellipses
Draw a series of ellipses of different sizes, maintaining a symmetrical shape and a constant distance between them.

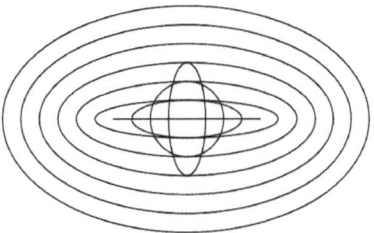

- Parallel ripples
Draw parallel wavy lines, maintaining an even distance between the lines. This exercise helps develop control and coordination.

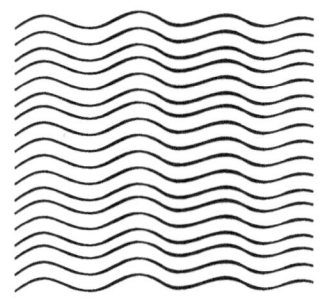

Chapter 2: observation and proportions

2.1 Observation active

Active observation is a crucial competence for improving drawing skills. Learning to see and interpret details accurately helps to reproduce what is seen more faithfully.

Learning to observe details

- Analysing form and structure

Start by carefully observing the general shape of the object. Try to identify its basic geometric shapes (circles, rectangles, triangles).

Exercise: Take a fruit, such as an apple, and try to visualise the geometric shapes that make up its structure.

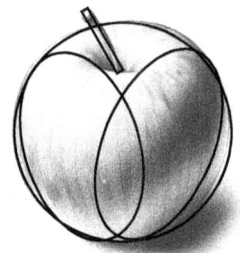

1. Start by drawing the basic shape of the fruit (a slightly irregular circle, etc.).
2. Add the veins, the petiole and any imperfections on the surface.

- Observe proportions

Study the relative proportions between the parts of the object. For example, note how the dimensions of one part relate to another.

Exercise: observe a coffee cup and note the proportions between the height and width, between the handle and the body of the cup.

1. Draw an oval to represent the upper edge of the cup.
2. Add vertical lines for the sides and another oval for the base.
3. Draw the handle, carefully observing its shape and where it connects to the cup.

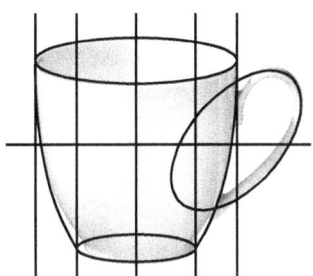

- Note the details

After outlining the basic shapes and proportions, it is important that you focus your attention on the smaller details, such as textures, shadows and reflections. Exercise: take a leaf and study veins, edges and colour variations.

1. Start by drawing the basic shape of the leaf, carefully observing the contours.
2. Add the main vein and secondary veins.

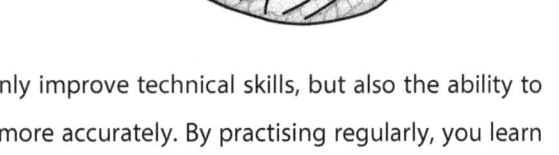

Life drawing exercises not only improve technical skills, but also the ability to see and interpret the world more accurately. By practising regularly, you learn to observe and capture details that you might otherwise miss.

2.2 The proportions

Study of proportions in basic forms

Understanding and respecting proportions is fundamental to creating realistic and balanced drawings. Proportions refer to the relative size of the parts of an object in relation to the whole. Through practical measurement and transposition exercises, you will learn to see and accurately represent the relative dimensions of objects. These skills are essential for all types of drawing, from portraits to landscapes, and form a solid basis for the next steps.

Proportions in geometric shapes
- Circle
A circle has uniform proportions in all directions, which means that the diameter is always the same, regardless of where it is measured.
Exercise: Draw a circle and check its proportions by measuring the diameter in different directions with a ruler.

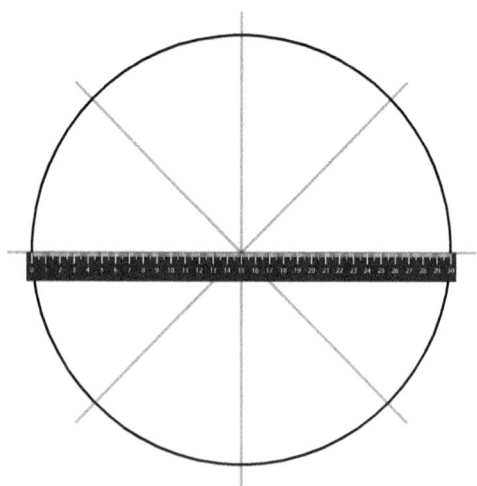

- Rectangle

A rectangle has two main dimensions: length and width.

Proportions refer to the ratio between these two dimensions.

Exercise: Draw rectangles with different ratios (e.g. 1:2, 2:3, 3:4).

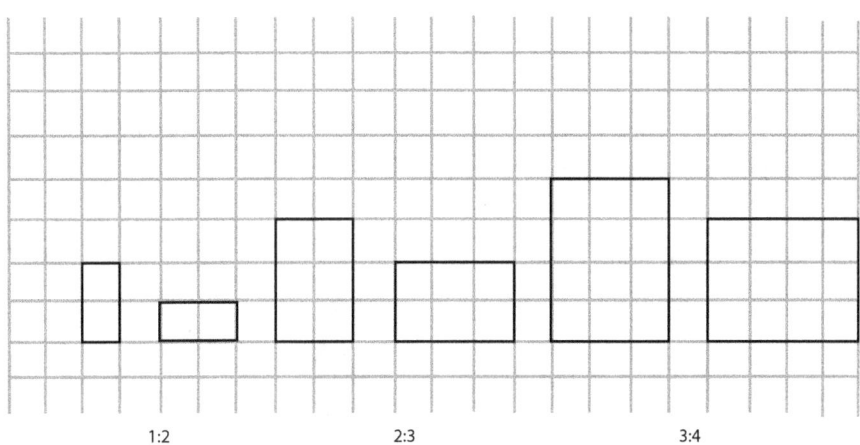

1:2   2:3   3:4

- Triangle

The proportions of a triangle depend on the length of its sides.

In equilateral triangles, all sides have the same length.

In isosceles triangles, two sides are equal, whereas in scalene triangles, all sides are different.

Exercise: Draw different types of triangles and study the proportions between their sides.

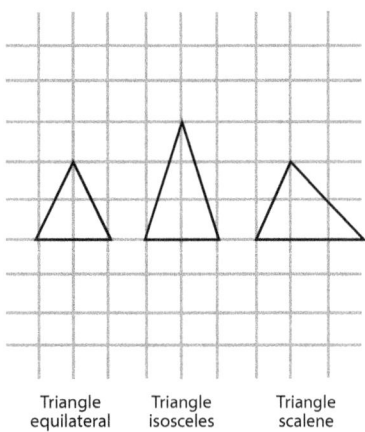

Triangle equilateral   Triangle isosceles   Triangle scalene

Exercises on how to measure and transpose proportions on paper

- Measuring with a pencil

Use a pencil to measure the proportions. Hold the pencil at arm's length, close one eye and align the top of the pencil with the top of the object. Use your thumb to mark the base of the object on the pencil. This will give you a reference measurement.

Exercise: Take a simple object, such as a bottle, and measure its height and width with a pencil (Fig.1). Transfer these measurements onto the paper to maintain the correct proportions (Fig.2).

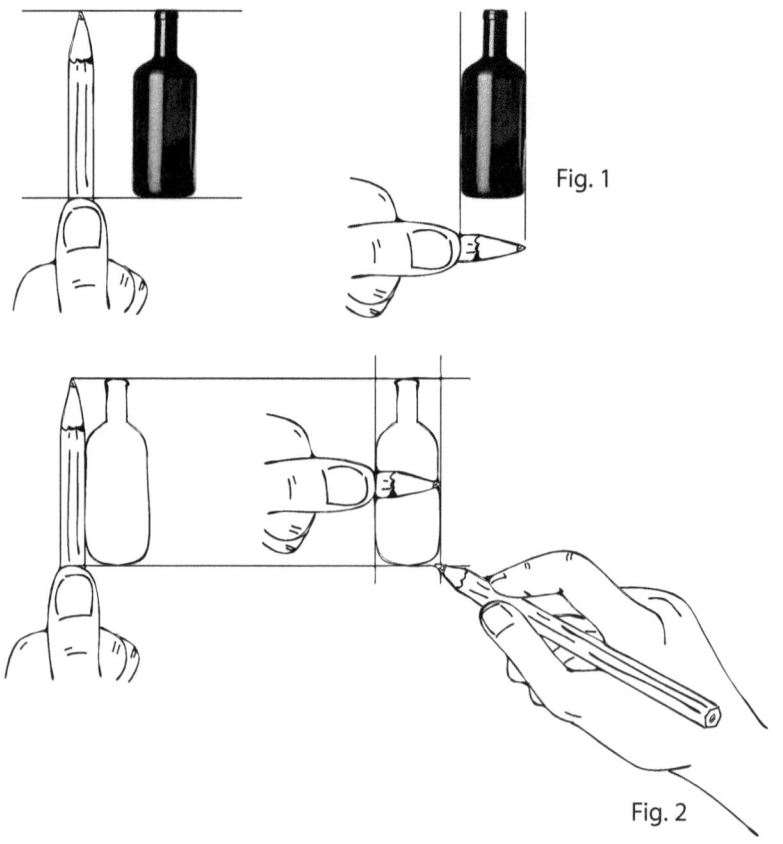

Fig. 1

Fig. 2

- Visual comparison

Usa parti dell'oggetto come unità di misura per altre parti dell'oggetto. Ad esempio, nota quante volte la larghezza di un oggetto si adatta alla sua altezza.

Exercise: Observe a complex object, such as a chair. Note how many times the height of the screen fits the total height of the chair (Fig. 1).

Draw the chair maintaining these proportions (Fig. 2).

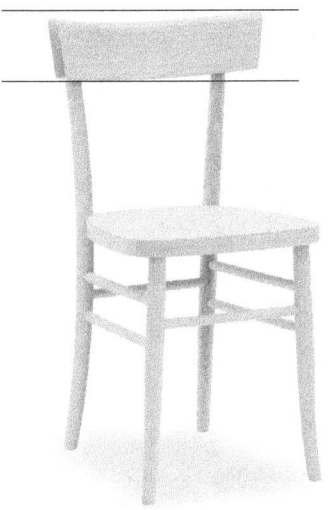

Fig. 1

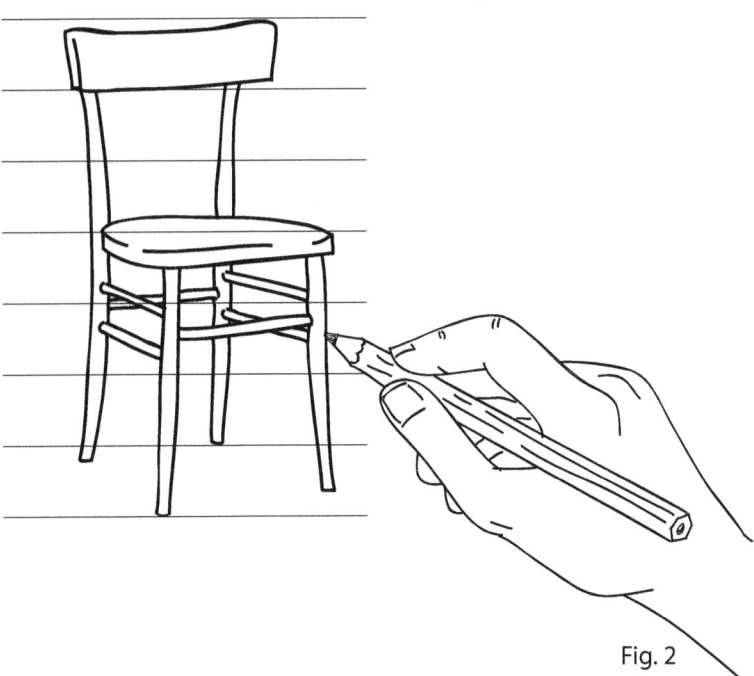

Fig. 2

2.3 The grid and the squares method

Using the grid to maintain proportions

The grid method is an effective technique for accurately transferring the proportions of an image. It consists of dividing the original image and the drawing sheet into a series of equal squares, using these grids as a guide to transfer the image onto the sheet.

By practising this method regularly, you will develop a sharper eye for detail and proportion, which will help you improve in all forms of drawing.

Steps for creating and using a grid

- Image preparation

1. Choose an image to reproduce.
2. Draw a grid on the original image. You can use a light pencil. (Fig.1).

- Preparing the drawing sheet

1. Draw a corresponding grid on your drawing sheet, making sure that the number of squares and the proportions are the same as in the original image (Fig. 2).
2. Use a pencil to trace the grid on the drawing sheet so that you can easily erase the lines after completing the drawing.

- Image transposition

1. Compare the corresponding squares between the original image and the drawing sheet.
2. Draw what you see in each square, paying attention to details and proportions (Fig.3).

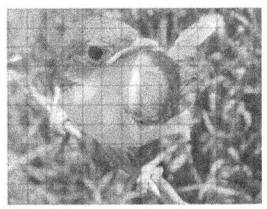
Fig. 1

Fig. 2

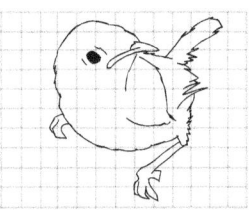
Fig. 3

Exercises in transposing an image using a grid Simple portrait

- Choose image

1. Select a simple portrait of a human face.
2. Draw a grid on the original image (e.g. 1 cm x 1 cm square) (Fig.1).

- Preparing the drawing sheet

1. Draw a corresponding grid on the drawing sheet. Always ensure that the squares have the same size and number as the original image (Fig.2).

- Transposing the image

1. Start copying the image square by square, paying attention to the lines and details in each square.
2. Complete the drawing making sure the proportions are correct (Fig.3).

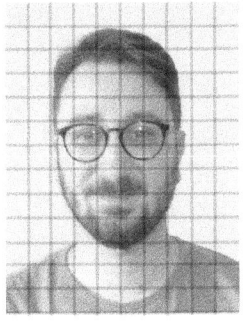
Fig. 1

Fig. 2

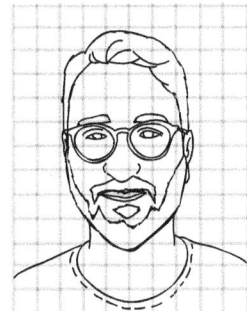
Fig. 3

Landscape

- Choose image

1. Select a simple landscape, such as a mountain or a country scene.
2. Draw a grid on the original image (e.g. 2 cm x 2 cm square) (Fig. 1).

- Preparing the drawing sheet

1. Draw a corresponding grid on the drawing sheet, with the same scale as the original image (Fig.2).

- Transposing the image

1. Copy the landscape square by square, carefully observing the position of lines, shapes and details.
2. Complete the drawing by checking the overall proportions (Fig 3).

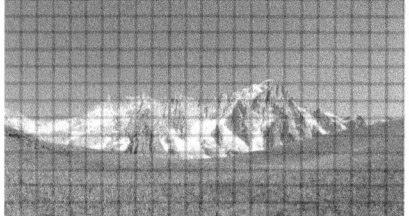

Fig. 1

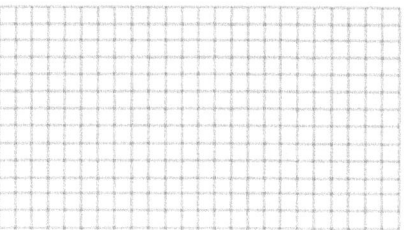

Fig. 2

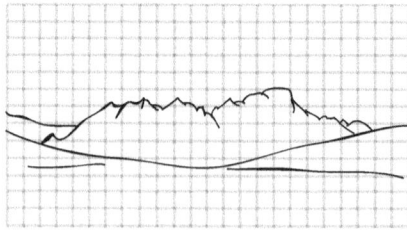

Fig. 3

Chapter 3: lights and shadows

3.1 Theory of light and of shadow

Understanding the theory of light and shadow is fundamental to creating realistic and evocative drawings. This part will focus on the basic concepts of light and shadow and how they affect objects.

With a thorough knowledge of the theory of light and shadow, artists can make their drawings more vivid and three-dimensional, adding depth and realism.

How light interacts with objects

- Sources of light

Light can come from different sources, such as the sun, a lamp or a candle. Each source has a different intensity and direction, which influence the appearance of the shadows.

- Reflection and absorption

When light strikes an object, it can be reflected, absorbed or transmitted. Opaque objects absorb light and create shadows, while transparent objects can transmit light through them.

Reflection, absorption and transmission of light are fundamental concepts that greatly influence visual perception.

- Light direction

The direction of light determines the arrangement of shadows and highlights on an object. Light directed from the front can create fewer visible shadows, while light from a side angle can produce more defined shadows.

Types of shadows: own shadows and brought shadows

- Own shadows

Own shadows are generated by the object itself when light is blocked or partially blocked by the object. Own shadows may vary in intensity, depending on brightness of the light source and the contrast between the object and the surface onto which they are projected.

- Shadows carried

Carried shadows are created when the light is blocked by the object and casts a shadow on a surrounding surface.
The shadows cast can be more long or shorter depending on distance between the object and the surface onto which they project.

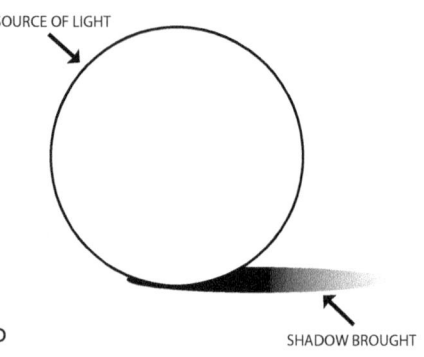

3.2 Shading of simple shapes

Shading and hatching techniques

The ability to shade simple shapes is essential for creating a sense of depth and volume in drawings. This part will focus on shading and hatching techniques that can be used to add realistic shading to geometric shapes.
Regular practice of these techniques on geometric shapes will provide a solid basis for shading more complex objects in the future.

Blurring and hatching

- Uniform blurring
This technique involves the uniform application of grey tones over an area to create a gradual transition effect from light to shadow.
Use a soft pencil or a graphite stick to apply darker tones in shaded areas and lighter tones in lit areas.

- Dot blurring
This technique involves the application of a series of small stitches to create a gradual fading effect.
Varies the density of points for create more or less intense shading.

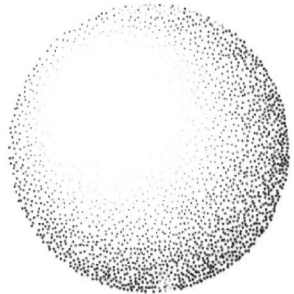

- Linear hatching

This technique involves the application of parallel or crossed lines to create shadows and textures.

Vary the length, thickness and orientation of the lines to achieve different effects.

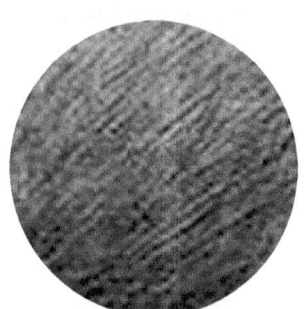

Practical exercises on geometric shapes

- Shading a cube

1. Draw a cube on a sheet of paper (Fig. 1).
2. Use shading and/or hatching techniques to create a realistic shading effect on the cube (Fig.2).
3. Focus on identifying shaded and lit areas and applying shading techniques accordingly.

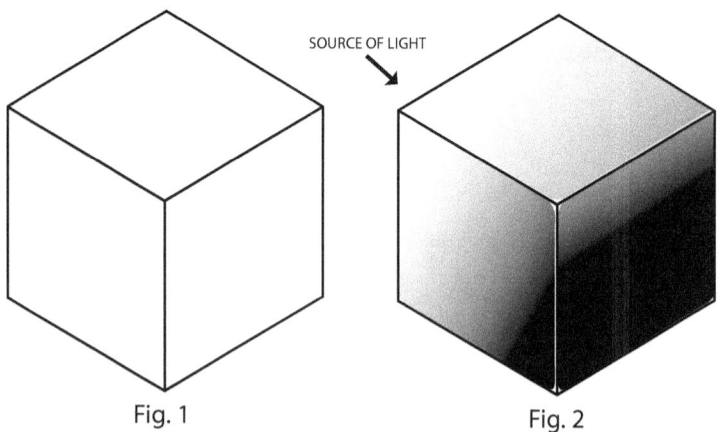

Fig. 1   Fig. 2

Shading a sphere

1. Draw a sphere on a sheet of paper (Fig.1).

2. Use shading and/or hatching techniques to create a realistic shading effect on the sphere (Fig.2).

3. Take the direction of the light into consideration and concentrate shading on areas where the light does not strike directly.

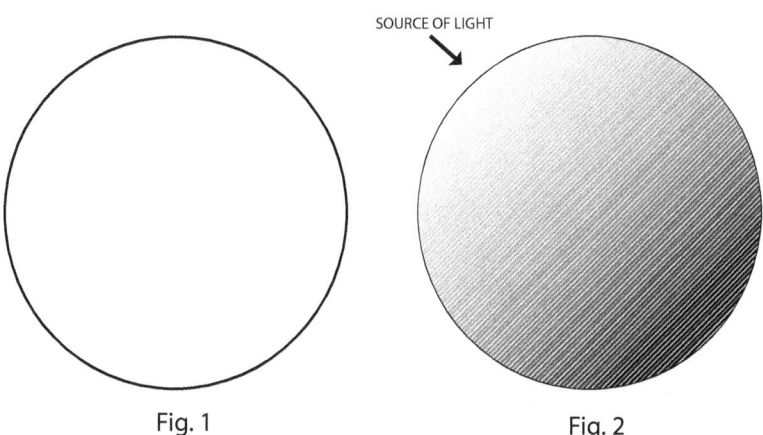

Fig. 1   Fig. 2

3.3 Volume and Depth

Creating the illusion of three-dimensionality

To make drawings more realistic and give them a sense of depth, it is fundamental to understand how to create the illusion of three-dimensionality. Using light and shadow techniques.

Basic Principles

- Chiaroscuro

chiaroscuro is the technique of using light and shadow to define shapes. Illuminated and shaded areas create contrast and make objects appear three-dimensional.

- Tonal gradation

Tonal gradation refers to the gradual transition between light and shadow. This technique is essential to create curved surfaces and to show volume.

- Perspective

Linear and aerial perspective help create the illusion of depth in space. Linear perspective is based on the use of vanishing lines, while aerial perspective uses changing tones and colours to suggest distance.

Practical exercises

- Cube

A cube can be drawn as a square with a trapezoid on top to give the impression of depth. Draw a cube and use chiaroscuro to shade it. Identify the light source and apply consistent shadows to each face of the cube.

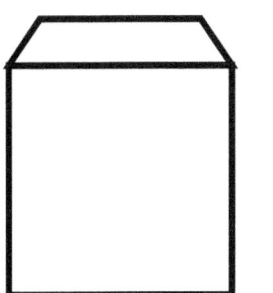 

- Sphere

A sphere is drawn as a simple circle. Draw a sphere and practise tonal gradation to create realistic shading.

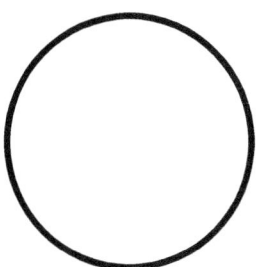 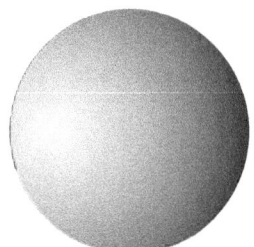

Drawing complex objects with light and shadow Complex objects

Once you have a good understanding of simple shapes, you can move on to more complex objects. The key to drawing complex objects is to break them down into simpler geometric shapes and apply the same techniques of light and shadow.

- Choose a complex object, such as a cup or bottle, and apply the techniques of chiaroscuro and tonal gradation.

Steps for drawing complex objects

- Analysis of basic forms

It identifies the basic geometric shapes that make up the complex object. For example, a cup can be divided into a cylinder and a ring (the handle) (Fig. 1).

- Sketch of basic shapes

Draw a simple sketch of the basic shapes to define the structure of the object (Fig. 2).

- Application of shadows

Identifies the light source and applies consistent shadows to every part of the object. Use chiaroscuro and tonal gradation techniques to render realistic shadows. Add details and finishing touches to complete the design. Pay attention to how light and shadow affect the smallest details (Fig. 3).

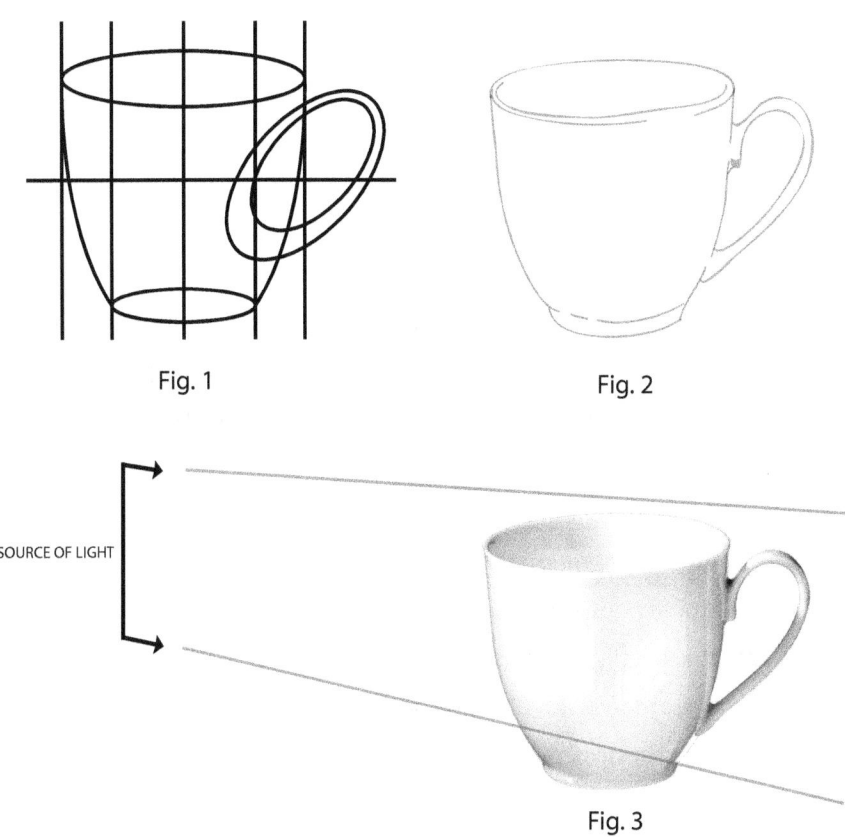

Fig. 1

Fig. 2

SOURCE OF LIGHT

Fig. 3

Chapter 4: perspective

4.1 Perspective linear

Basic concepts of perspective (vanishing point, horizon line)

- Vanishing point

The vanishing point is a crucial concept in linear perspective. In a perspective drawing, parallel lines extending into space appear to converge towards a point called the vanishing point. This point represents the observer's point of view or the distant infinity towards which the lines are heading. In one-point perspective, there is a single vanishing point on an imaginary horizon line.

- Horizon line

The horizon line is an imaginary line representing the eye of the observer or the eye level of the observer. In a perspective drawing, this line usually crosses the image horizontally. The position of the horizon line determines the point from which the observer is looking at the scene.

In one-point perspective, the horizon line is parallel to the ground plane and is usually drawn at the observer's eye level.

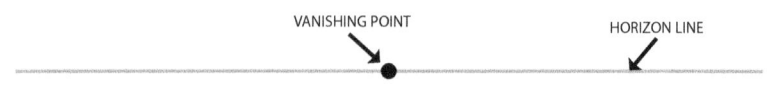

Drawing shapes in perspective

Drawing shapes in one-point perspective means representing three-dimensional objects on a two-dimensional surface using a common vanishing point. This type of perspective is often used to create a sense of depth in drawings and paintings. When drawing shapes in one-point perspective, the lines converge towards the vanishing point.

A classic example of single-point perspective drawing is to draw a cube in which all lines start from the vanishing point.

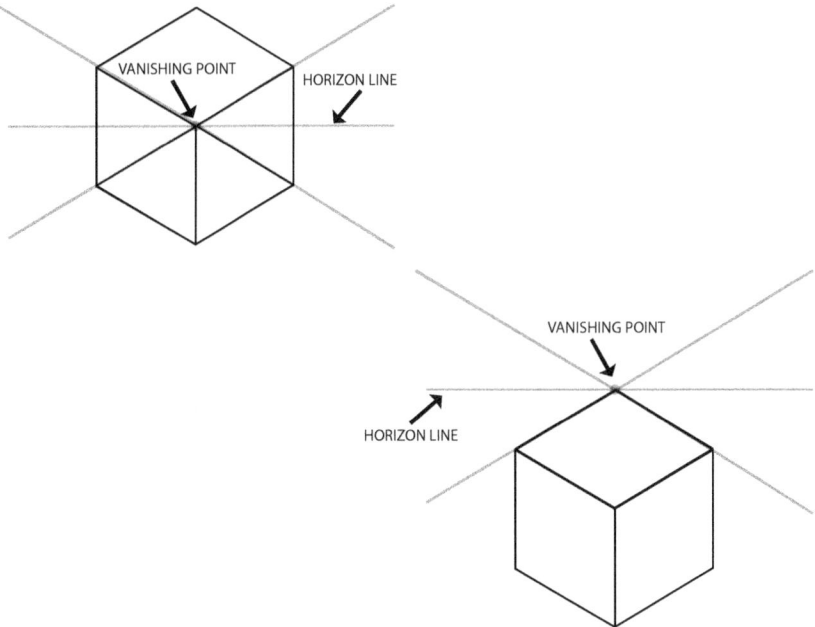

By combining these concepts, it is possible to create realistic drawings that give the illusion of depth and space on a flat surface. This is a fundamental aspect in the art of illustration, architectural drawing and spatial representation in general.

4.2 Two-point perspective points

Two-point perspective is a fundamental technique in drawing that allows three-dimensional objects and environments to be represented on a two-dimensional surface, creating a sense of depth and realism. In this part, we will explore the practical application of two-point perspective and learn how to draw more complex objects and detailed environments.

Application of two-point perspective

Two-point perspective is based on two vanishing points that are located on the horizon. These vanishing points are used to draw all lines heading towards the horizon, creating an illusion of depth.

- Horizon line

This line represents the observer's eye level.

- Escape points

Two points on the horizon line to which all parallel lines converge.

Step 1: Draw the horizon line and vanishing points

Start by drawing a horizontal line (horizon line) on the sheet. Place three vanishing points on this line, one in the centre, one on the left and one on the right, and draw three vertical lines passing over the three vanishing points.

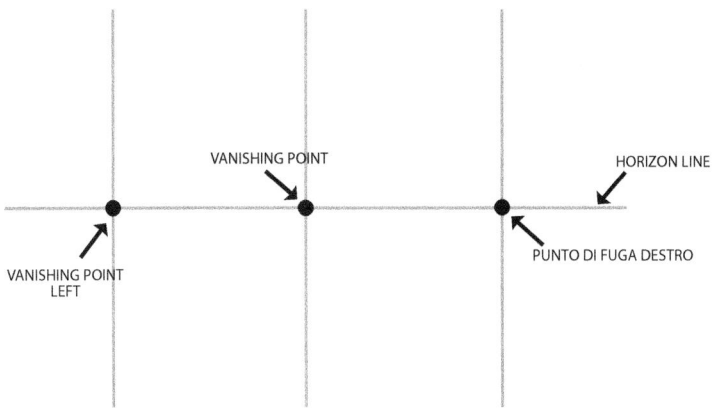

Step 2: Draw guidelines

Draw guide lines from the central vanishing point to the vertical lines of the two vanishing points, both upwards and downwards.

Then draw from the two vanishing points (left and right) two lines that converge true to the vertical line of the central vanishing point.

These lines will define the size and shape of the object.

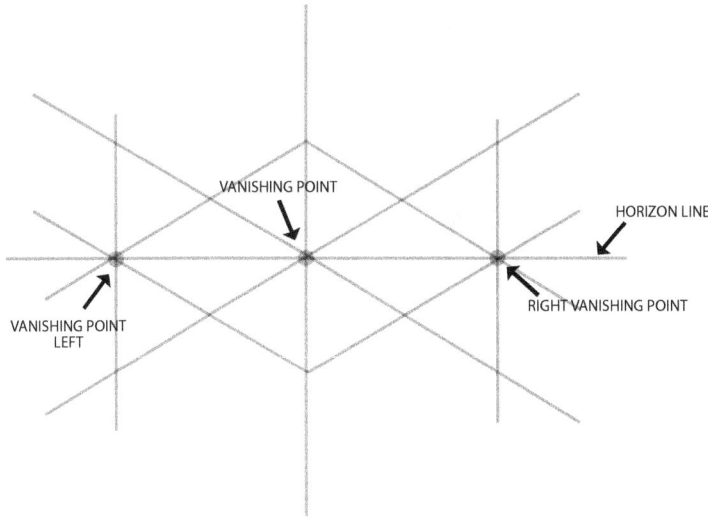

Step 3: Build the object

Use the guide lines to draw the contours of the object.

The horizontal lines of the object converge towards one of the vanishing points, while the vertical lines remain parallel to each other.

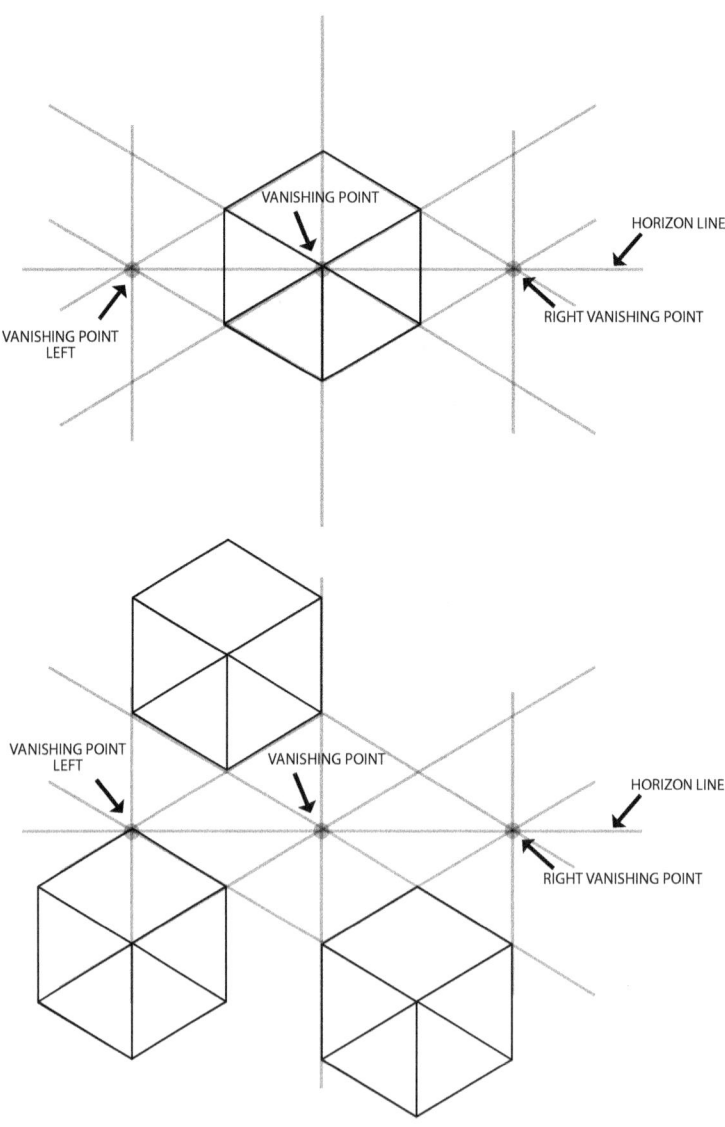

Drawing complex objects and environments Drawing a building

1. Base of the building: draw the base of the building as a rectangle that converges to the vanishing points.
2. Adding details: draw windows, doors and other details, ensuring that all horizontal and vertical lines converge correctly.
3. Roof perspective: for the roof, draw additional guide lines converging towards the vanishing points to create the illusion of depth.

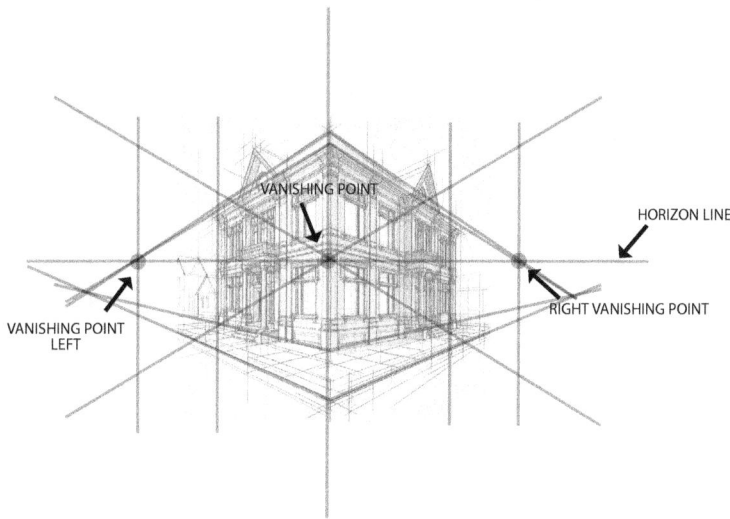

Creating a complete environment

1. General outline: draw a general outline of the environment, such as a street with buildings on either side.
All elements must follow the rules of vanishing point perspective and two-point perspective.
2. Adding details: add details such as trees, street lamps and people, make sure that all elements respect the vanishing points.
3. Lights and Shadows: Add lights and shadows to increase the realism of the scene.

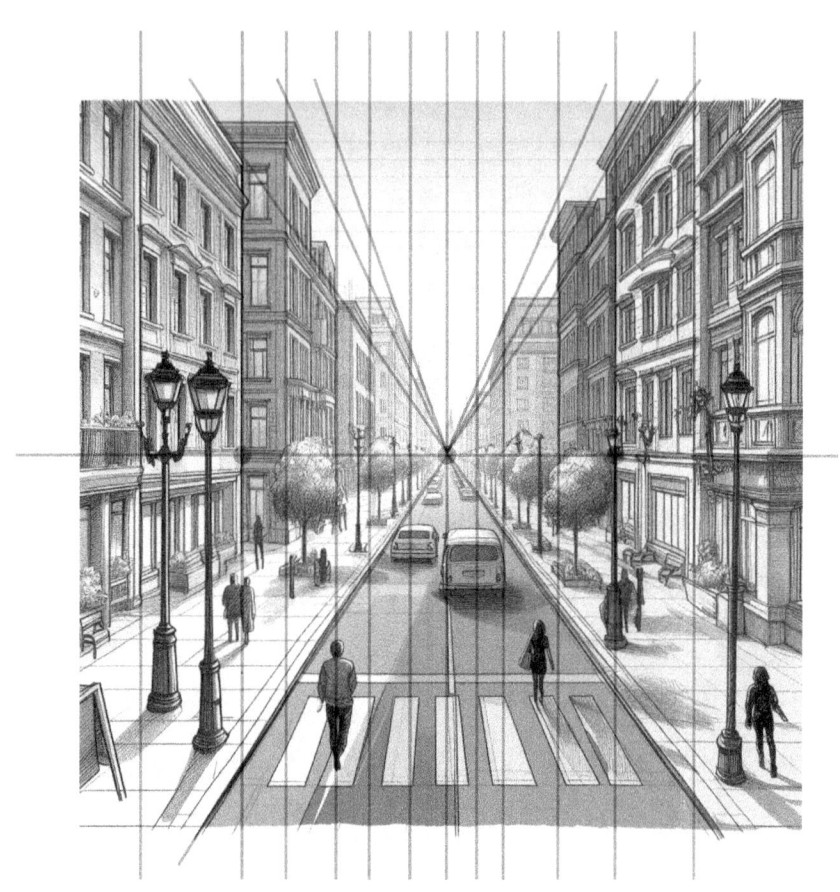

4.3 Perspective atmospheric

Atmospheric perspective, or aerial perspective, is a technique used to create the illusion of depth and distance in drawings and paintings.

This technique is based on the observation that distant objects appear less sharp and bluer or greyer due to the effect of the atmosphere.

We will explore how to use tonal values to create depth in your drawings, with a focus on practical exercises with landscapes.

Using tonal values to create depth

- Tonal values: lighter values represent the illuminated areas, while darker values represent the shaded areas. In the atmospheric perspective, closer objects have a wider tonal range and stronger contrasts, while more distant objects appear lighter and with less contrast.

- Blurring and sharpening: Near objects are more detailed and sharp, while distant objects are more blurred. This effect is achieved by reducing details and softening the contours of distant objects.

- Colours and saturation: atmospheric perspective not only affects tonal values, but also colours. Nearby objects have more saturated and vivid colours, while distant objects appear more desaturated and tend towards blue or grey.

This phenomenon is caused by the scattering of light in the atmosphere.

Practical exercises with landscapes

To fully understand atmospheric perspective, it is useful to practise with landscapes, where the effect is particularly evident.

Exercise 1: Mountainous landscape

- Preparation

Take a reference photo of a mountainous landscape, preferably with several planes of depth (e.g. a series of mountains receding into the horizon).

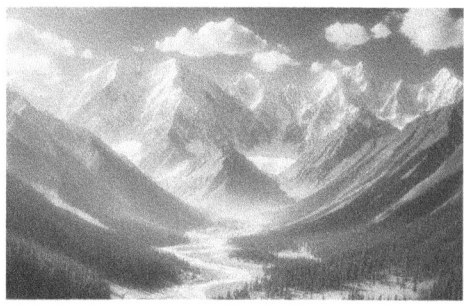

- Initial sketch

Make a quick sketch of the main contours of the landscape. Don't worry about the details at this stage.

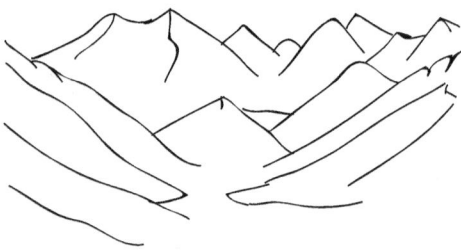

- Tonal values

Use greyscale to define tonal values. The closest mountains should have the darkest tonal value and sharp details. The more distant mountains should be clearer and less detailed.

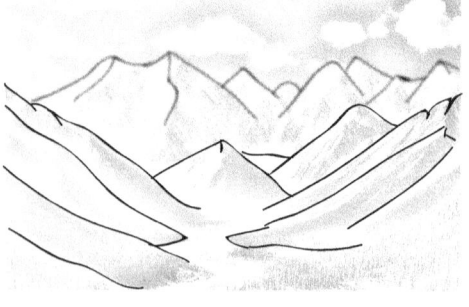

- Blurring and sharpening

Slightly blur the contours of distant mountains to create the effect of distance.
Keep the contours of nearby mountains sharp and detailed.

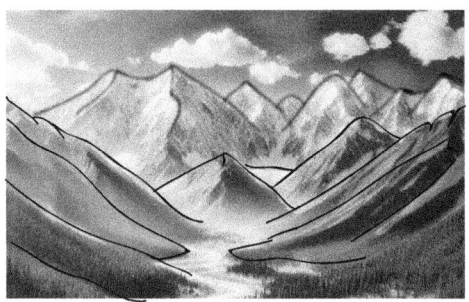

- Colouring (if applicable)

For a colour drawing, use more saturated colours for the neighbouring mountains.

Reduce the saturation and add a blue or grey tone for distant mountains.

Exercise 2: Urban Landscape

- Preparation Select a photo of reference of an urban landscape with various buildings stretching towards the horizon.

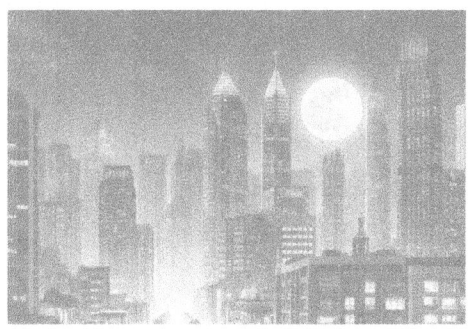

- Initial sketch

Draw the main contours of the buildings.
Focus on the general composition.

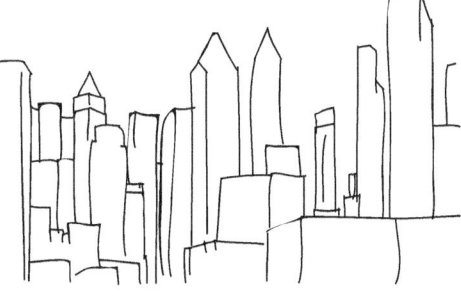

- Tonal values
Nearby buildings should
have darker shadows and
highlights brighter.
Far away buildings will have a
average tone value,
with less contrast.

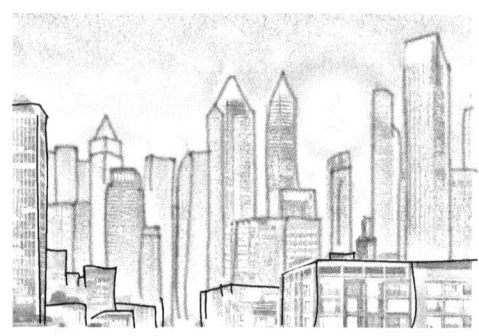

- Blur and sharpness
Slightly blurs them
buildings in the distance.
Detail nearby buildings
with precision.

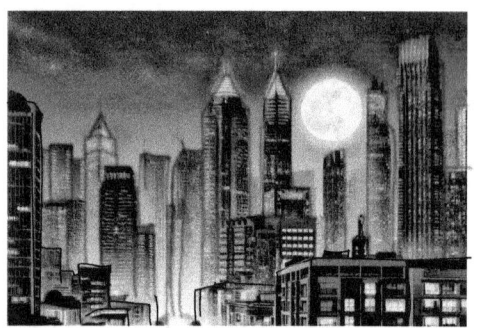

- Colouring (if applicable)
Use bright colours for neighbouring buildings.
Desaturate colours and add a slight darker tone for distant buildings.

Practical advice
Direct observation
Spend time observing real landscapes. Notice how colours and details change with distance.

Experimentation
Don't be afraid to experiment with different techniques and tools. Try different combinations of tonal values and colours to see what works best.

Chapter 5: Drawing Objects and Nature still life

5.1 Drawing of everyday objects

Object and still life drawing is an important discipline in the visual arts, focusing on the accurate representation of inanimate objects and compositions of natural or manufactured elements. This part is dedicated to the drawing of everyday objects, focusing on the analysis of textures and details of common objects, as well as performing practical exercises aimed at developing technical skills.

Study of textures and details

Textures are the surface characteristics of objects that define how they appear and how they interact with light. In drawing everyday objects, you will learn to observe and represent a wide range of textures, which can include metal, ceramics, fabric, wood, paper, plastic, among other materials. Understanding how to draw these textures requires detailed observation skills and mastery of drawing techniques to render realistic surface differences.

In addition to textures, details include specific elements such as reflections, wrinkles, cracks, scratches, wear marks and other unique features of objects. Attention to detail is crucial to make objects convincing and realistic in design.

Exercises on everyday objects

Practical exercises can include several methods.

- Direct observation

Observe objects around you carefully, noting not only their general shape but also their most minute features.

- Study of light and shadow

Practice drawing objects under different light sources to understand how lighting affects the perception of textures and details.

- Texture analysis

Exercises can focus on specific objects to explore how to draw and render different textures, using pencils, charcoals, pastels or other drawing techniques.

- Artistic composition

Create compositions of everyday objects that not only exercise drawing skills but also have artistic aesthetic value, considering the balance, arrangement and interaction of objects in the composition.

Importance of the exercise

These exercises not only help develop technical drawing skills, but also improve the ability to observe and understand the physical characteristics of objects. The drawing of everyday objects and still life also serves as a basis for learning fundamental artistic techniques, preparing one to handle more complex challenges in portrait, landscape and conceptual art.

5.2 Composition of a still life

A still life is a type of painting, drawing or photograph depicting inanimate objects, such as fruit, flowers, household utensils, and other everyday objects. Here are some key concepts.

Composition and balancing of elements

Composition

Composition refers to the arrangement of objects within the painting. A good still life composer seeks to guide the viewer's eye through the painting in an interesting and meaningful way. Some common principles of composition include:

- Focal point

A focal point can be a main object or an area that immediately attracts attention. Placing the focal point at a strategic point can make the composition more dynamic.

- Rule of thirds

Dividing the image into horizontal and vertical thirds and placing the main elements along these lines or at their intersections can create visual balance.

- Balance

Balance refers to the visual distribution of the weight of objects within the image. There are two main types of balance.

In symmetrical balance, objects are arranged symmetrically about a central axis, creating a feeling of stability and calm.

In asymmetrical balance, objects are arranged non-symmetrically, but the visual weight is distributed equally, creating a dynamic and interesting balance.

Balancing the elements

Element balancing refers to the visual distribution of objects so that no part of the image looks heavy or empty. There are several ways to balance a composition.

It is possible to use colour, shape, size or light and shadow contrasts to balance objects within the image.

Repeating shapes, colours or patterns can create a sense of cohesion and balance the image. Organising objects so that some are more emphasised than others can help establish a visual hierarchy and balance the composition.

Drawing of a still life with various objects

When drawing a still life, it is important to consider:

- Selecting Objects

Choosing interesting and varied objects can enrich the composition.

Objects can have symbolic or aesthetic significance.

- Arrangement of objects

Experimenting with different arrangements of objects before starting to draw can help you find the most effective composition.

- Light and shadow

The management of light and shadow is crucial for making objects three-dimensional and realistic. It helps to create atmosphere and depth in the image.

- Materials and artistic techniques

Choosing the right materials and techniques depends on the desired result. For example, pencils, pastels, watercolours or mixed techniques can be used to create different visual effects.

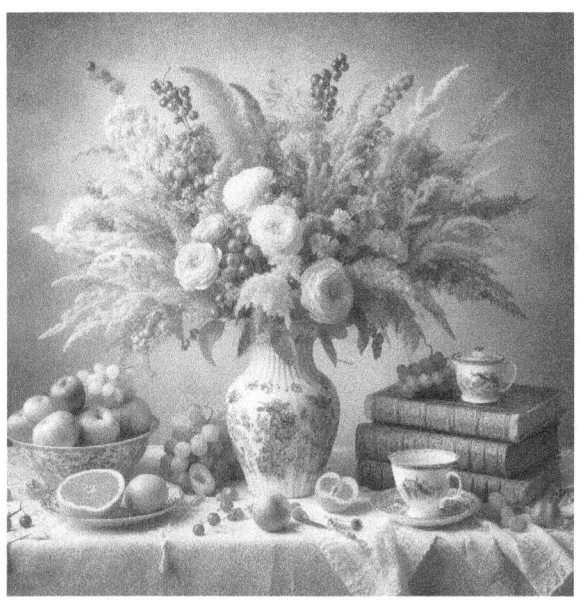

In summary, the composition of a still life is not only about the arrangement of objects, but also their visual relationship, the balance of elements and the creative use of light and shadow. These principles help transform an everyday scene into a meaningful and aesthetically pleasing work of art.

5.3 Colour in nature dead

The use of colour is very important in the depiction of still life. Colour plays a fundamental role in still life, as it can add depth, realism and emotion to the artwork.

Introduction to colours and colouring techniques

Colour theory is essential for understanding how pigments work, colour combinations and how they interact in visual representation. Artists need to know the concepts of hue, saturation, luminosity and the colour wheel to create a balanced and harmonious palette.

Colouring techniques can vary from delicate nuances to bolder and more vibrant applications, depending on the desired effect.

Using colour to enhance drawing

Colour can be used to emphasise shapes, create contrast, suggest depth and convey emotion. For example, the use of warm colours such as red and orange can add warmth and vitality to still life, while cool tones such as blue and green can give a feeling of coolness and tranquillity. Furthermore, the careful choice of colours and their arrangement can guide the viewer's eye through the composition and create a sense of visual balance.

Improving drawing through colour requires practice and experimentation to achieve effective results.

Artists must consider light and shadow, perspective and the size of objects in order to apply colour realistically and convincingly. The skilful use of colour can transform a simple still life into a vibrant and engaging work of art.

Chapter 6: design of the human body

6.1 Anatomy of base

In this section we address two topics crucial to the successful representation of the human body: correct anatomical proportions and the drawing of stylised figures.

Human body proportions

The proportions of the human body are crucial to creating realistic and believable drawings. Artists must understand how the different parts of the human body relate to each other in terms of size and ratios, as this affects the overall appearance of a figure. For example, the human head is often used as a unit of measurement to determine the proportions of the whole body. Knowing the correct anatomical proportions helps artists avoid distortions and make figures more realistic.

The proportions of the human body are an important topic in the science of anatomy and art. This concept has been studied by various artists, scientists, physicians and anatomists throughout history to accurately represent the human body in artistic works or to better understand the structure and functioning of the human body.

One of the best-known measures used to establish the proportions of the human body is the so-called 'canon' of Vitruvius. Leonardo da Vinci's Vitruvian man represents the canon of perfect human proportions according to the writings of the Roman architect Vitruvius. According to Vitruvius, there are specific ratios and ideal measurements for the correct proportions of the human body. Leonardo da Vinci relied on these proportional canons to create his famous drawing, which inscribes the human body in a circle and a square, symbolising the centrality of man as the measure of all things.

The drawing shows the human body in a central position, with arms and legs extended, inscribed in a perfect geometric figure, representing the harmony of Vitruvian proportions.

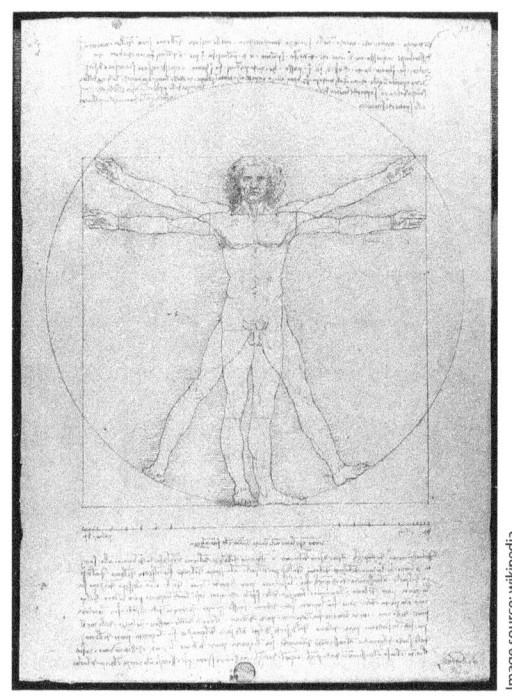

Other approaches to determining human body proportions include the use of relative measurements, e.g. the head as the unit of measurement for the whole body. According to this method, an average person is approximately seven to eight heads tall. Human body proportions vary from person to person due to factors such as age, gender, genetics and ethnic background. However, there are some general proportions that are considered aesthetically pleasing and harmonious. For example, shoulder width is usually about twice the width of the pelvis, and leg length is often about half the total height.

Step-by-step drawing of a human body in proportion

Drawing a human body in proportion can be facilitated by using the head as a unit of measurement. This method is very useful to ensure that the various parts of the body are in proportion to each other.

Steps for drawing a female body

Head and spine

1. Draw an oval for the head.
2. Draw a vertical line down from the head to represent the spine.

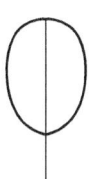

Shoulders and chest

1. Draw a horizontal line about two heads wide by the shoulders.
2. Draw an oval to represent the chest.

Navel and pelvis

1. Draw a horizontal line about three heads from the top of the head to the navel.
2. Draw an oval under the chest, about a head and a half wide, for the pelvis.

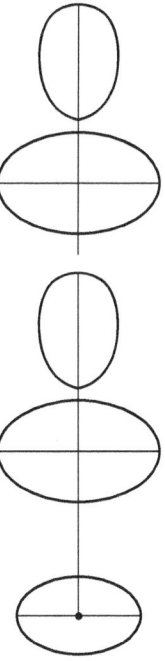

Arms

1. Draw the arms extended to about three and a half heads from the shoulder.

2. The hands should be about half the length of the head.

Legs and feet

1. The thighs, from the top of the femur to the knee, are about two heads long.

2. The legs, from knee to ankle, are about two heads long.

3. The feet are about half a head wide.

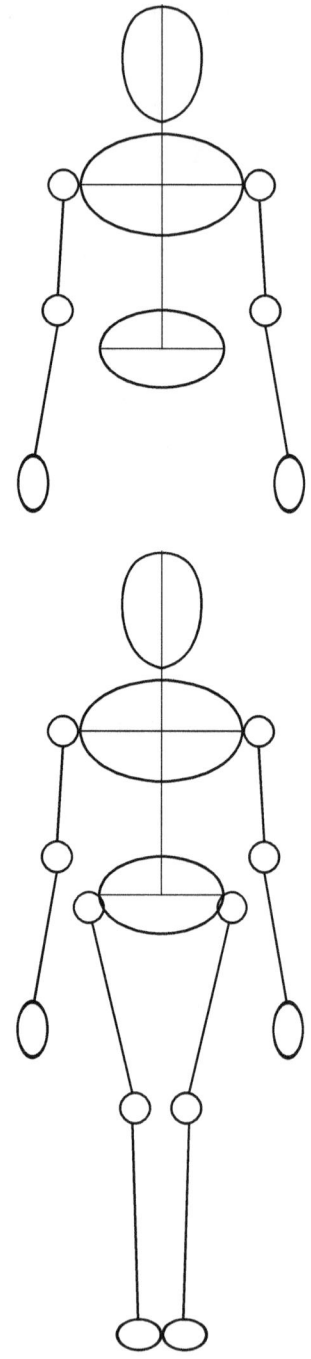

Steps for drawing a male body

Head and spine

1. Draw an oval for the head.
2. Draw a vertical line through the centre of the circle and down.
This will be the guide for the spine.

Pelvis and shoulder line

1. Draw an oval for the pelvis, positioned about four heads below the top of the head.
2. Draw a horizontal line for the shoulders, which will be about two to three heads wide.

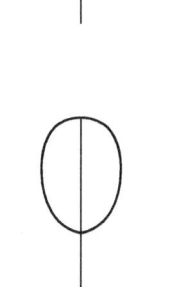

Chest

1. Draw a wider oval to represent the chest, around the shoulder line.

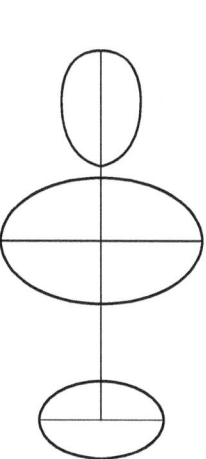

Arms

1. Draw the arms extended to about three and a half heads from the shoulder.
2. The hands should be about half the length of the head.

Legs

1. The thighs, from the top of the femur to the knee, are about two heads long.
2. The legs, from knee to ankle, are about two heads long.
3. The feet are about half a head wide.

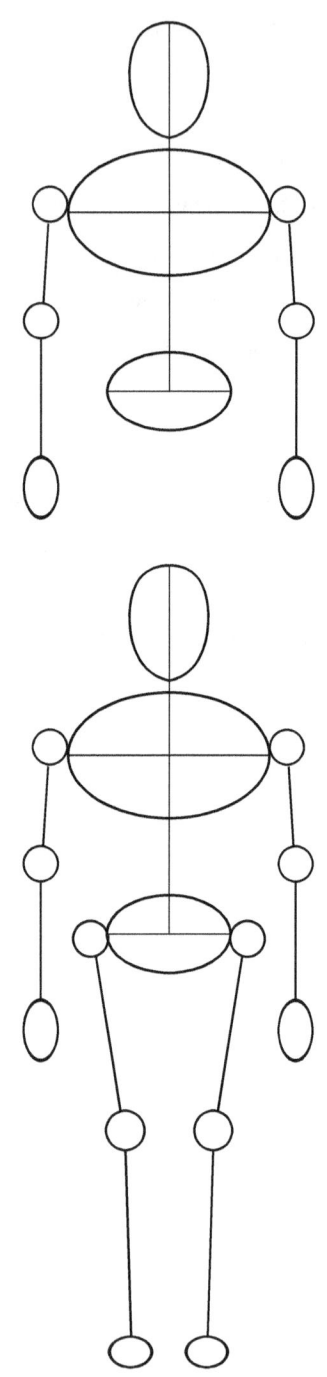

Drawing of stylised figures

Stylised figure drawing involves simplifying or altering the proportions and features of the human body to create a unique and stylised artistic aesthetic. This approach allows artists to express concepts or emotions in a more abstract and creative way, breaking away from traditional realistic representations. Stylised figures can be used to bring fantastic characters to life, illustrate symbolic concepts or simply add personality to drawings.

This type of drawing is an artistic approach that consists of representing human forms or objects in a simplified and exaggerated manner, often distorting proportions and details to create an essential or emblematic interpretation of reality. This drawing style is commonly used in art, graphic design, animation and visual communication to express concepts, emotions or ideas in a distinctive and original manner.

In stylised figure drawing, the artist attempts to capture the essence or distinctive character of a subject by reducing its features to simple shapes and clear lines. This may include the elimination of non-essential details, the accentuation of particular physical features or the use of geometric shapes and stylised patterns to represent the subject.

Stylised figures can be used to communicate complex concepts in an immediate and direct manner without overloading the observer with unnecessary visual information. This type of drawing is widely used in the creation of icons, logos, comics, cartoons and contemporary art illustrations.

In the creation of stylised figures, the artist has the freedom to interpret and manipulate the shapes and proportions to his or her liking, thus creating a unique and recognisable style. This artistic approach allows the artist to explore creativity and experiment with new forms of expression, contributing to the development of a personal and distinctive visual language.

Drawing stylised figures requires a good understanding of the proportions and basic structure of the represented subject, as well as an artistic sensitivity to communicate effectively through simplified forms.

This artistic style can be a source of inspiration and a versatile medium for exploring creativity and expressing ideas in a unique and appealing way.

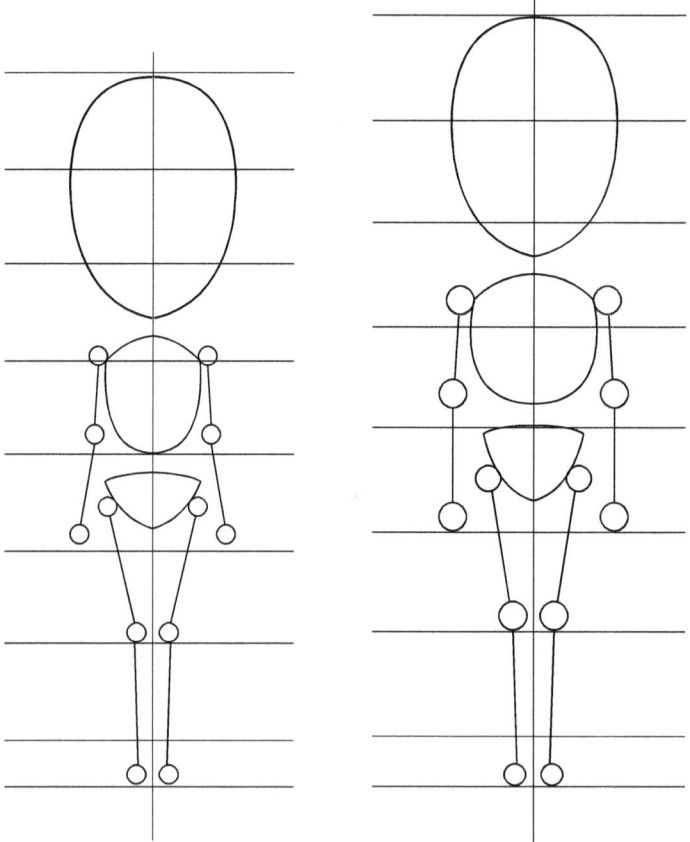

Example of a female stick figure   Example of a male stick figure

6.2 Study of the parts of the body

The study of human body parts is crucial for artists, who seek to understand the structure and characteristics of these parts for different purposes. Here are some focal points related to the study of human body parts.

Drawing of hands, feet and face

The hands, feet and face are body parts that are often difficult to draw due to their anatomical complexity and the many expressions they can assume. Artists carefully study the proportions, details and movements of these parts to create realistic portraits and figures.

Practical exercises for every part of the body

These exercises may include freehand drawings, proportion studies, relief exercises, quick sketching techniques, study of facial expressions, hand and foot movements, and more. For example, artists can do exercises drawing hands in different poses and expressions.

To improve mastery in the drawing of hands, feet and face, it is advisable to carry out a series of targeted practical exercises.

Hands

To draw the back of the hand, we can use the division into two main blocks: the palm/back and the fingers. By following a simple geometric structure, we can ensure that the proportions are correct.

1. Drawing the back of the hand
- Shape of the back: draw an irregular hexagon to represent the back of the hand. This hexagon should be wider at the top (near the fingers) and narrower at the bottom (near the wrist) (Fig.1).

2. Drawing fingers
- Positioning the fingers: divide the upper back into five sections to represent the finger bases (Fig.1).
- Finger joints: draw the fingers as segments that align in a succession of lines. Each finger has three phalanges (segments), except the thumb, which has only two (Fig.1).

3. Finger refinement
- Finger phalanges: Add detail to the fingers by drawing the three phalanges (segments) for each. The thumb, on the other hand, will only have two phalanges (Fig.2).
- Nails: add nails as small curved shapes on the tip of each finger (Fig.2).

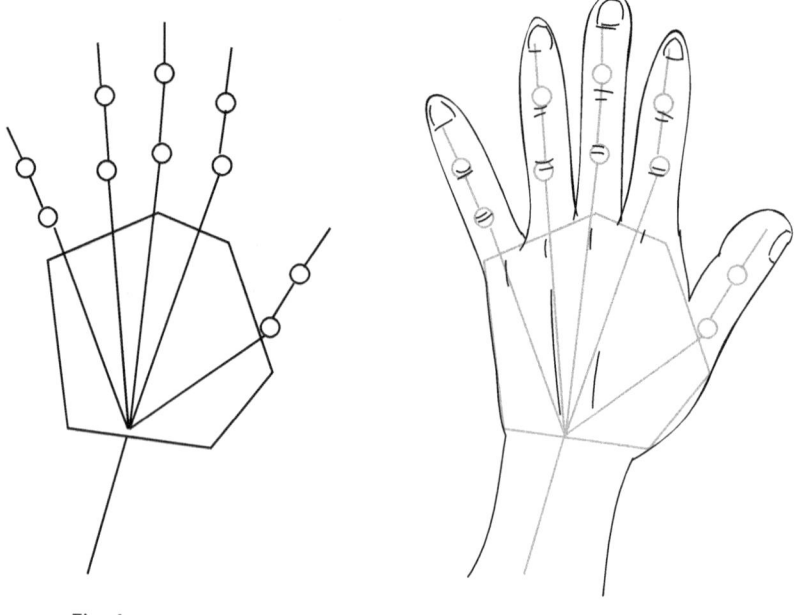

Fig. 1   Fig. 2

1. Drawing the palm of the hand
- Basic shape: draw an irregular hexagon representing the palm of your hand. The corners and sides do not have to be perfectly equal; the important thing is to obtain a shape that vaguely resembles a hexagon.
- Centre of the palm: marks a central point within the hexagon. This will be useful to position the fingers and to represent the rectangle representing the carpus (Fig.1).

2. Drawing fingers
- Finger joints: draw the fingers as segments that align in a succession of lines. Each finger has three phalanges (segments), except the thumb, which has only two (Fig.1).

3. Refine your fingers and thumb
- Finger shape: add the shape of the fingers around the lines. Remember that the fingers are wider at the base and narrow towards the tip (Fig.2).

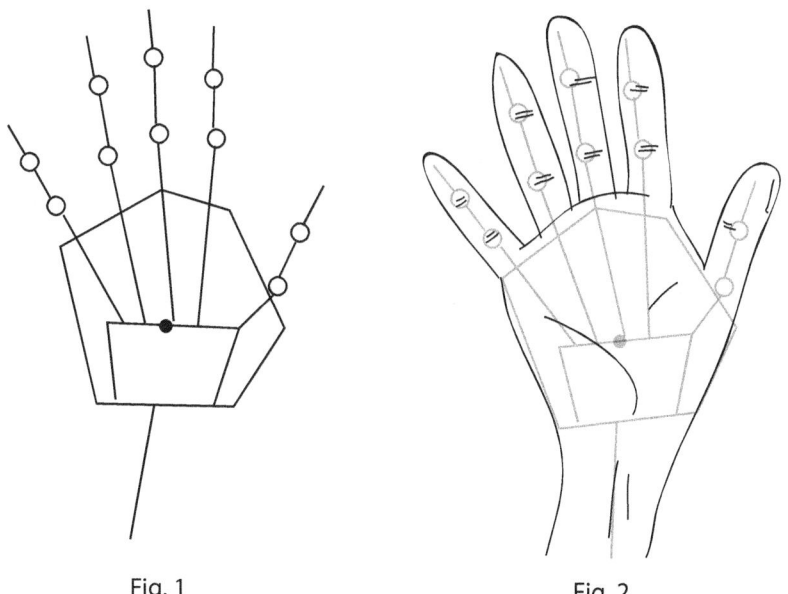

Fig. 1   Fig. 2

Follow these structures by drawing your hands in various positions.

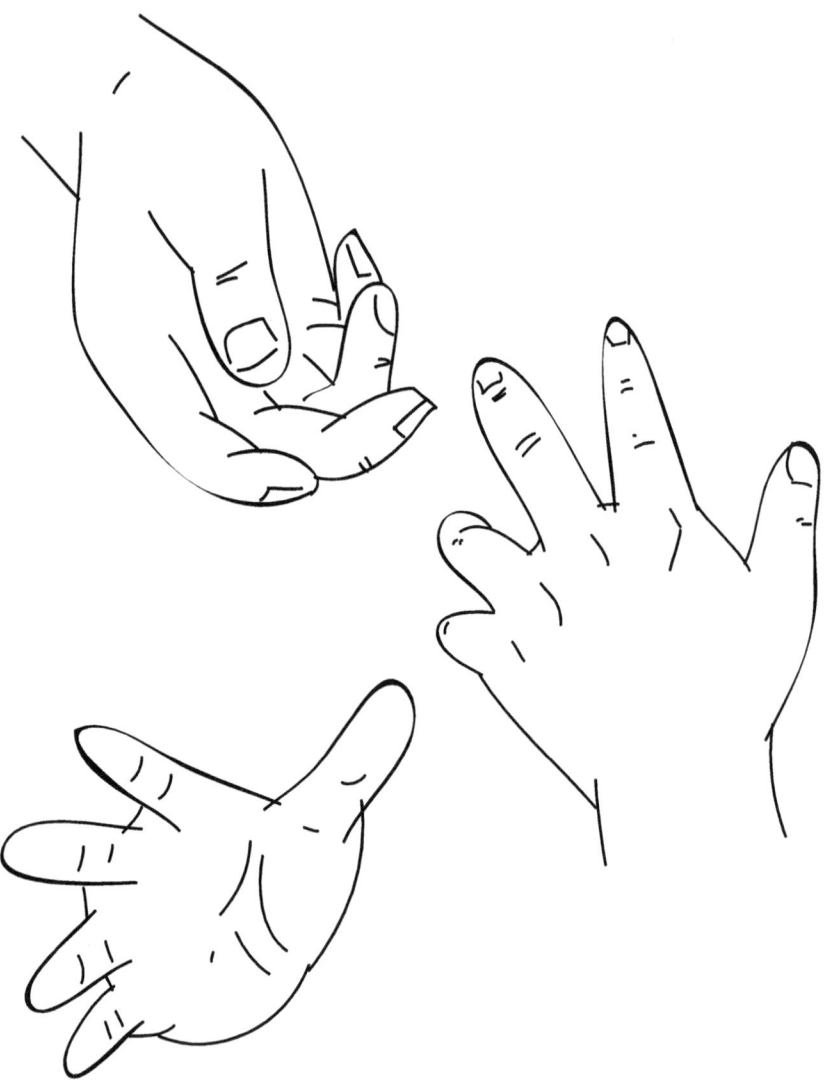

Feet

View from below

Drawing feet seen from below requires special attention to the pads that protect the joints and the general shape of the sole of the foot. Below, I will guide you step-by-step through the process of drawing feet from this perspective.

1. Draw the basic shape

- Basic shape: start by drawing an elongated, oval shape representing the shape of the foot. This shape should be narrower towards the heel and wider towards the toes (Fig.1).

- Divide the oval into sections representing the toes, arch and heel (Fig.2).

2. Add bearings

- Finger pads: Draw small ovals in the front to represent the pads under the fingers (Fig. 2).

- Heel pad: draw a large oval in the back for the heel pad (Fig2.).

- Plantar cushion: design an oval for the plantar cushion (Fig.2).

3. Detail areas

- Inner area: highlights the area inside the foot that does not touch the ground, i.e. the plantar arch (Fig.3).

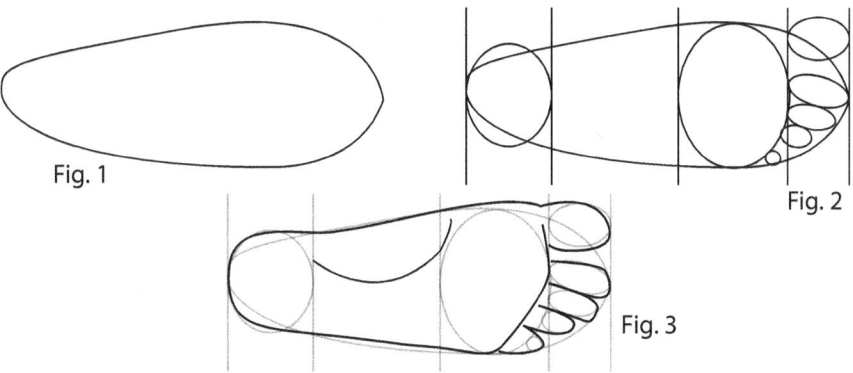

Fig. 1

Fig. 2

Fig. 3

View from above

To draw the feet from a top-down view, we need to understand their structure and shape. The feet tend to widen towards the toe and the toes are aligned in a descending arch. We can divide the foot into three distinct volumes: tarsus, metatarsus and toes. Furthermore, each toe has three phalanges except the big toe which has two.

1. Draw the basic shape

- Basic shape: start by drawing an elongated 'pear' shape representing the foot. The narrowest part represents the heel and the widest part represents the toe area (Fig.1).
- Divide into sections: divide the 'pear' into three sections to represent the tarsus, meta-tarsus and fingers (fig. 2).

2. Add fingers

- Fingers: Draw a descending arch that aligns the fingers. Remember that the big toe has two phalanges, while the other fingers have three (Fig.2).
- Finger segments: draw segments for each finger (Fig.3).

3. Detailing the areas of the foot

- Tarsus and metatarsus: add details to the volumes of the tarsus and metatarsus (Fig.4).
- Fingers: refine the shape of the fingers by adding joints and phalanges (Fig.4).

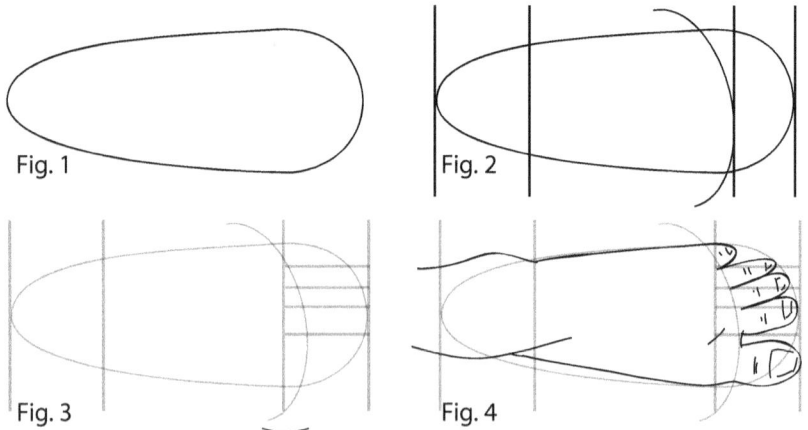

Fig. 1

Fig. 2

Fig. 3

Fig. 4

Follow these structures by drawing your feet into various positions.

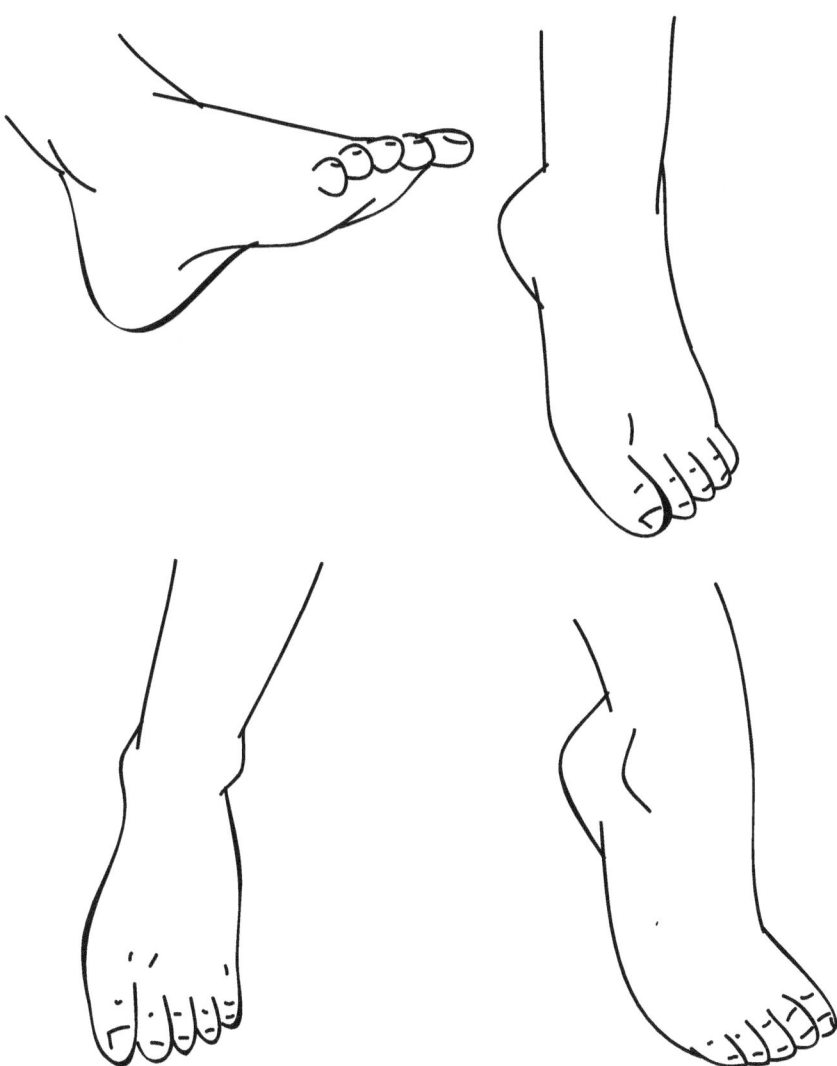

Face

Drawing a face in front view requires a basic structure to ensure symmetry and correct proportions. Here is a step-by-step guide.

1. Draw the basic structure
- Circle of the head: draw a circle representing the top of the head (Fig.1).
- Chin line: extend a vertical line from the centre of the circle downwards to define the length of the face (Fig.1).
- Add a curve to the base to represent the chin, thus creating a kind of oval (Fig.2).

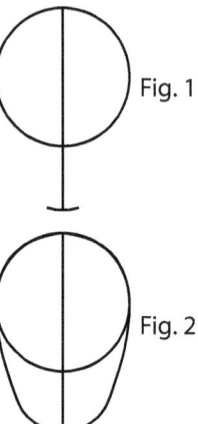

2. Guidelines for eyes, eyebrows, nose and mouth
- Eye and eyebrow line: divide the oval in two halves with a horizontal line. This will be the eye line. Above this draw another line, this will be the eyebrow line.
- Nose line: divide the lower part of the oval into two equal parts with a horizontal line. This will be the nose line.
- Mouth line: further divide the lower part of the oval (below the nose line) into two parts with a horizontal line. This will be the mouth line.

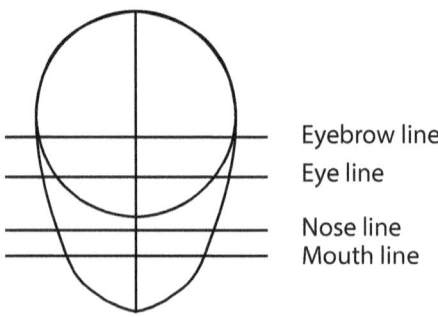

3. Position the eyes, nose and mouth

- Eyes: draw two ovals along the lines of the eyes.

- Nose: draw the nose along the nose line, centred vertically.

- Mouth: draw the mouth along the line of the mouth, with the corners coinciding with the centre of the eyes.

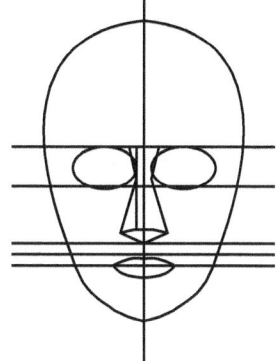

4. Place your ears

- Ears: the ears are located between the eyebrow line and the base of the nose.

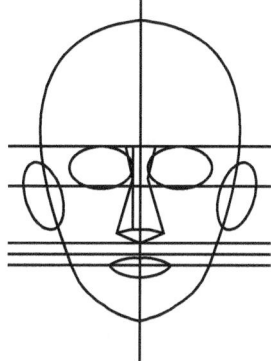

Drawing a face in 3/4 vision

Drawing a face in 3/4 vision requires a slightly different approach to frontal vision, as you have to consider the angle of the face. Here is a step-by-step guide to help you realise your drawing.

1. Head shape

Start with a light circle to represent the top of the head (Fig.1).

Draw a curved vertical line across the circle according to how you want the face to be tilted.

This line represents the axis of the face (Fig.1).

Add a curve to the base to represent the chin (Fig.1), thus creating a kind of oval (Fig.2). This oval will be the base on which to build the rest of the face.

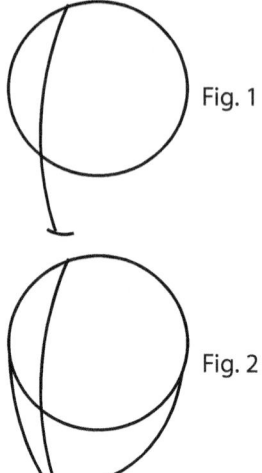

Fig. 1

Fig. 2

2. Eye line

Draw a slightly curved horizontal line across the circle,

placing it at the top to mark the position of the eyes.

Remember that in 3/4 vision, the eye line will not be perfectly horizontal,

but slightly curved to fit the perspective.

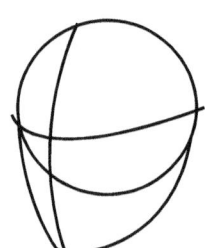

3. Positioning of facial elements

Considering the angle,

draws guidelines for the nose and mouth.

The nose will be positioned laterally in relation to the central axis, the mouth will follow the same logic.

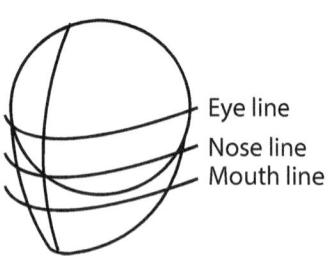

Eye line
Nose line
Mouth line

4. Eyes and ears

The eyes will be positioned on the eye line, but consider that the eye on the visible side will be larger and more detailed than the eye on the opposite side. Draw an oval to represent the ear, will be placed approximately in the middle of the nose line.

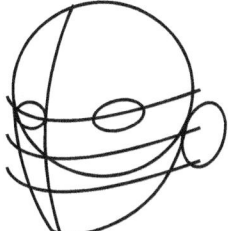

5. Details and finish

Add details such as eyebrows, lips and other distinctive features of the face. Be sure to emphasise depth by using tones and shadows to define the shape of the face and make the 3/4 perspective realistic.

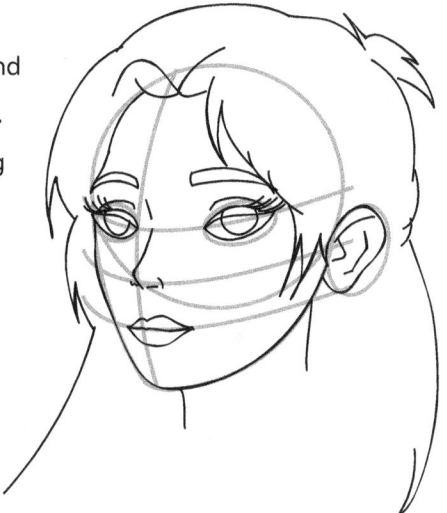

6. Finishing

Check that the proportions are correct and that the design reflects the desired angle. Make any necessary adjustments to balance the perspective and ensure that the face appears consistent and proportionate.

6.3 Figures in movement

Drawing dynamic poses

The drawing of dynamic poses is an essential element in the artistic representation of human movement. Let us take a look at some key points that further explore this topic.

Expression of movement
Dynamic poses allow artists to capture the action and energy of human figures in ways that convey a sense of movement and vibrancy. Drawing lines and shapes are used to express fluidity and dynamism, providing viewers with an engaging visual experience. Through studied and well-realised poses, artists can create works that convey a sense of action and vitality.

Studying the movement of the human body
A fundamental aspect in the design of dynamic poses is the in-depth study of the movement of the human body. Artists spend time observing the way the body moves in different activities and situations. This study helps them to understand the fluidity of movement and to represent it accurately in their drawings. Direct observation, the study of photographs or videos and detailed analysis of body movements are all methods used to improve the representation of movement.

Creating tension and movement
Dynamic poses are able to communicate tension, action and emotion to their viewers. Through the use of lines, shading and contrasts, artists can create visual compositions that effectively convey the feeling of movement and energy.

The choice of postures, focal points and expressions can help to make the human figures more realistic and engaging, thus capturing the viewers' attention.

Study of movement and balance
The study of movement and balance is essential to represent the human body accurately and realistically. Here are a few important points that go into this topic.

Movement and space management
Familiarising oneself with the principles of movement and spatial management is important for creating dynamic and realistic representations. Knowing how the body moves in three-dimensional space, the direction of movement, rhythm and fluidity of gestures are crucial aspects for capturing the essence of movement in works of art. Understanding how to distribute weight and maintain balance through correct posture contributes to the credibility and naturalness of moving figures.

Muscle strength and tension
Understanding muscle tension and muscle contraction during movement is crucial to bringing the drawn figures to life. Artists must study how muscles activate and relax during various actions and poses in order to accurately portray muscle tension and the energy of movement. Knowing which muscle is responsible for a particular action helps to make the illustration more believable and realistic.

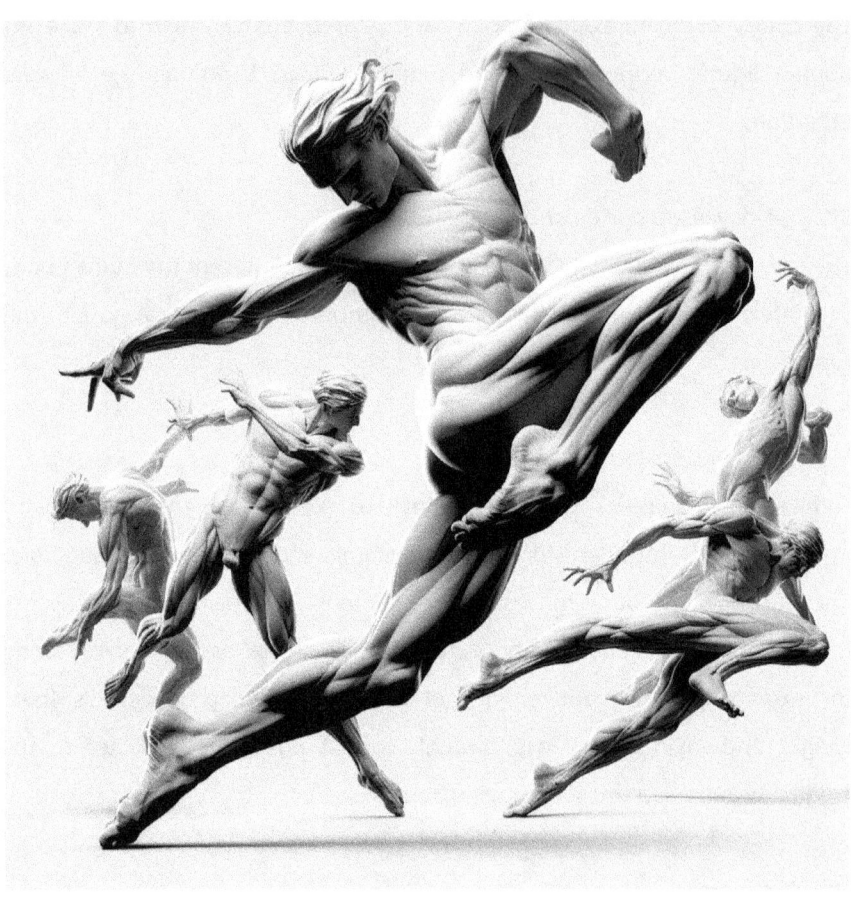

Through practical exercises, anatomical study and observation of people in motion, artists can hone their skills in drawing dynamic poses and representing movement and balance in their art. By combining creativity with a sound understanding of the mechanics of movement, works can be created that convey energy, emotion and life to the figures depicted, thereby enhancing the quality and impact of artistic creations.